CONTENDING FOR YOUR DESTINY

Finding Your Purpose Through Life's Trials!

Pam

Healing is in your story. You will bring Healing to many through your transparency and openess to share what God did in your life. I pray that my book blesses you!

CYNTHIA B. JACKSON

2016

CONTENT

FOREWORD

If you are someone that has questioned God's plan for your life, *"Contending For Your Destiny"* is a must read. The author uses practical life examples of how she overcame rejection, fear and failure by giving her testimony and applying the word of God to each situation and circumstance. She helps the reader to understand what it takes to go from trial to triumph.

No matter what your life looks like now - if you have ever thought about giving up, if you have felt that you must please other people, or you just want to be all that God has predestined you to be, *"Contending For Your Destiny"* will certainly give you the tools to help you achieve your full potential in Christ Jesus.

Cynthia Jackson knows how you can become victorious in your life. She knows how to take the word of God and apply it to every circumstance that you may be faced with. Most of all she knows how to fight with the weapon of the word.

With her testimony and using the principles from the scriptures, your life can change forever! Cynthia Jackson did and she wants to show you how. In this book you will learn:

*How to overcome rejection

*How God has a perfect plan for your life

*How to deal with past hurt and fear

*That your covenant with God will never be broken

*That God will never leave nor will He forsake you

When you apply the word of God to life's battles, you will be amazed at your outcome. You win!

Minister April Sansbury
Harrisburg, PA

FOREWORD

The Lord brought Cynthia into my life in 2004. During this time, I was in the midst of my own trials and had fallen victim to the lies and schemes of the devil. Not unlike many women in today's fallen world, I already had a child out of wedlock at the age of 20. Much like Cynthia, I also knew the Lord at a young age. What I did not know was the power I had already been given through Jesus Christ to engage in the spiritual warfare that would be necessary to defeat the enemy's attacks on my God-given destiny. Cynthia, through her commitment to God and her commitment to help others find their destiny in the Lord, encouraged me to press into Jesus Christ. She encouraged me to seek the Lord in order to find the purpose for my life through Him and used her gift of prayer to provide me spiritual cover from the enemy as I grew in the Lord. Of course Cynthia did this not in her own power, but through the power that resides in her as the Lord Jesus Christ lives in her. She listens to the prayers that the Spirit reveals to her to engage in on behalf of others. She allows herself to be used by the Lord for His purpose even when it makes no sense. I can testify that I have seen the

Lord work through her time after time!

Cynthia's obedience to God and her determination to keep her promise to serve the Lord, allowed her to be used by Him to save another child of God from the lies of the enemy. That child of God was me. I thank the Father for Cynthia's trials that revealed her power and purpose in God and I thank the Father for my own trials and tribulations that have led to my understanding of my purpose to be used by the Lord Jesus Christ to do works for the Father.

We are all children of God who have been saved in the resurrection of Jesus Christ and who have the wisdom provided through the Holy Spirit to contend for our destiny! I pray this book will be a blessing to you as Cynthia's presence in my life has been a blessing for me. God is Great!

Georgia Erimee

Servant of the Most High God-Jehovah

Mechanicsburg, PA

INTRODUCTION

We are all created for a purpose! We are not here on earth just taking up space, and we shouldn't wait on others to fulfill our purpose and destiny in Jesus Christ. There are assignments that God has called us to do that involve using our spiritual gifts, talents and warfare strategies to contend with the enemy for the manifestation of His promises in our life and the lives of others.

"Contending for Your Destiny" is the title the Lord gave me for this book because I believe before we can truly live the life that God has ordained us to live, we have to get a revelation knowledge and understanding of what it takes to remain in the presence of God and receive strategies to overcome the schemes and plans of the enemy. Our contending is with principalities, powers, rulers of darkness of this age and spiritual hosts of wickedness. (Ephesians 6:11-12). Their assignment is to attempt and successfully steal our focus, faith and dedication to Jesus Christ. Our assignment is to make it difficult and impossible for them to fulfill their assignment by being fully committed to our Lord and Savior Jesus Christ through our obedience to His Word. Our destiny is secure in Christ and we are saved by believing that He came to this earth, died for our sins, and is sitting at the right hand of God making intercession for us, but we have to know that there are specific God assignments that will require us to contend with the demonic spiritual forces that may be preventing us from fulfilling our destiny in Christ. Just as Jesus heard His Father's voice and was obedient, we too must hear the voice of God and be obedient. When Jesus lived on the earth, he had opposition and distraction coming at Him from all directions, but He did not allow these things to keep Him from pursuing and fulfilling His assignments. Jesus was able to use the Word of God to expose the tactics of the enemy so that He could fulfill His assignments here on earth and redeem us from the power of sin. Jesus walked through situations that were designed to destroy Him. He knew His purpose and destiny and through the leading of our Heavenly Father, was victorious even unto death.

We contend from a place of rest and obedience, not from a place of striving. This battle is not ours and God will fight for us. His Grace is sufficient for us; however, there are strategic moves and positions in certain seasons of our lives that God requires us to be in. While in these seasons, the Holy Spirit teaches us how to reinforce our offensive position against the enemy's tactics, plots and plans. It is my prayer that as you read this book, you would allow the Holy Spirit to minister to you regarding your destiny and also reveal how to contend in the spirit realm for yourself and for those in your sphere of influence for generations to come. Jeremiah 29:11 says, *"For I know the thoughts that I think toward you"*, **says the Lord,** *"thoughts of peace and not evil, to give you a future and a hope."* We have hope in the Lord. It is through His word and by the leading of the Holy Spirit that He reveals to us every spiritual weapon we need to do battle against the devil and walk in our calling - fulfilling the destiny and purpose that Christ has for us. We can fight and win!

ACKNOWLEDGMENTS

First of all I want to thank our Lord and Savior Jesus Christ for holding me together in times when I was falling apart. Jesus showed me that I was worthy of living and that He has purposed and called me to be used as an instrument to the Body of Christ for His Glory. I also want to thank my husband for being patient with me through my personal trials; my wonderful sons, James and Jaryn and my beautiful mother, Minister Betty Jean Baker for always being there for me in all situations

DEDICATION

I would like to dedicate this book to all the women in my life but especially to my mother, Minister Betty Baker.

Thank you for all that you have done for me, I realize that we can choose who we desire to be our friends but God has strategically ordained you as my mother and for this I am grateful. Thank you.

THE BEGINNING

I can recall the first time that I gave my life to the Lord; I was around 13 years old. My sister and her boyfriend had an encounter with a man of God on our street. He ministered the Word of God to them and they gave their lives to the Lord that night. When they arrived back to the house, they were crying, praising God and speaking in tongues. I joined them in prayer and gave my life to the Lord. That night a weight was lifted off of me. I was thirteen so I was not aware of the bondage that I was in. All I know is that I felt free, and what I now know to be a 'burden' was lifted off of me. The next day I went to school and told my science teacher Mr. Green, who was also a believer, that I had given my life to the Lord. At that time I did not know what all of this meant, but what I did know was that I felt different. It was like my heart was more attentive to God. I did not want to do what the other girls were doing. When other girls were experimenting with sex, cutting school and getting into trouble; I didn't, because the desire was not in me to do those things. I was very quiet growing up, so I would not say much but I thought a lot - which I believe allowed me to hear the voice of the Holy Spirit.

I would love to tell you that from that point on, I was sold out for the Lord. However, this was not so. My life was plagued by insecurity, low self-esteem and fear. Not knowing what the root causes of these feelings were, I just accepted them as just being who I was. However, I have since come to the revelation knowledge that this was a spiritual attack on my purpose and destiny. My mother had her first child when she was 16, her second child at 17, her third child at 19 and me when she was 21 years old. She also went on to have two more children; my younger brother and sister. My mother's second child Paula, died when she was just 22 days old. By the time my mother was 26, she had given birth to six children. This still amazes me because I cannot imagine having had six children at the age of 26 and raising all of them by yourself. My father was a married man when I was conceived. He already had a family when he and my mother entered into a relationship. I am not judging my mother. We all have done things in our life that we are not proud of and it is only by the Grace of God that we are here today standing as we are standing. Although my mother had an affair with a married man, she took care of all her children and still does to this day - including her grandchildren.   When my father rejected my mother and went back to his wife, I was an infant. I believe it was at this point that the spirit of rejection entered into my life and had the opportunity to try and derail God's purpose and destiny for my life. But God! He had the better plan for my life. He eventually revealed to me that I was not an unwanted child, but I was ordained to be here on earth. According to Jeremiah 1:5, **"Before God formed me in the womb He knew me, and before I was born He sanctified me"**. So I say to all who are reading this book, it is not about how you were conceived, but what is most important for you to know is that God knew you before you entered into your mother's womb. He has justified you - making you free of blame and sanctified you, setting you apart for a work just as He did for Jeremiah. We are all fearfully and wonderfully made (Psalm 139) and we need to embrace this truth. We have purpose!

My mother was a single parent and did the best she could to raise five kids by herself, so talking about our destiny and purpose was not something that she did. She was working hard to give us everything we needed in the natural and at that time her main priority was keeping a roof over our heads and food on the table. What she did do was expose us to Jesus by taking us to church, reading the bible to us and telling us how she and her grandmother would pray when she was young. What she gave to us was exposure to Jesus and that is better than any designer jeans or shoes that were popular in the 1990's. I now realize that what she exposed us to had an impression on all of her children, because we all know the Lord. With that being said, she taught us about having faith in God, but we had to learn on our own how to activate our faith in Jesus. I had no clue on how to activate my faith in Christ. I did not know that I could ask Him to reveal His Purpose for my life. The founder of Starbucks, Howard Schultz had an interview with Oprah Winfrey. During this interview he said, "Just having faith is not strategic". I allowed what he said to really minister to me. I thought what he said made sense. Just saying you are something or will achieve something in your life will not automatically make it happen. Confessing it opens your mind to conceive it, but there is much work that you have to do to bring it to pass. Whatever that "Work" is, you will have to couple it with your faith and move step by step to see it come to pass. You can have faith - but if you don't activate your faith with works, nothing will manifest in your life. According to James 2:14 it says, *"What does it profit, my brethren, if someone says he has faith but does not have works?"* (NKJ) I had faith but did not know how to activate my faith. James 2:17 goes on to say, *"Thus, faith by itself, if it does not have works is dead."* If you know what God has called you to do, then walk it out and allow God to reveal each step of the way to you. If you were like me and really did not know what God called you to do, just ask Him to reveal it to you. Some of us have the answer right before our natural and spiritual eyes, but we have allowed distractions to come and hinder us from seeing what God has called us to do. I just want to encourage you today by saying, you are a gift and God has given you gifts and talents that are apart of who He has created you to be and do. Don't think for one moment that your life is insignificant. You mean so much to the Lord and He died so that you can live the best life here on earth. You are special and God has wonderful things in store for you.

I remember right before my eighteenth birthday, I was getting ready to graduate high school and my mother said to me, "Once you turn eighteen, you will have to find you a job because I will not be receiving support for you any longer". I was so afraid. I was afraid because I had no clue of what my purpose was or what I was going to do. I had no aspirations of what I wanted to become. I was insecure and fearful. I recall listening to some of my fellow graduates saying how they were going to go to college and get a degree in a specific career field and thinking, at least they had an idea. I did not even have an idea so needless to say, I felt even more inferior and inadequate. I was clueless of what it was that I wanted to do with my life. So I signed up for the Army. 'Yes, this is it', I thought - or at least at that time it was what I wanted to do. But I soon came to find out that it wasn't. I signed up for the Army in May of 1990. I went through the medical process only to find out that because I had a heart mummer, I could not join the military. When my recruiter found this out, he did not accept that report. I remember him saying, "I am going to send you back and the next time you tell them you are ok". So being young and not having an idea of what I wanted to do with my life, I went back through the medical process and did exactly what my recruiter instructed me to do and I passed. I was to leave for boot camp in October of that year. I remember the entire summer thinking I didn't want to go into the Army. These thoughts would come and go. Finally, one day I was in the kitchen with my mother and she asked me, "Do you not want to go into the Army"? I said "No". She said, "Tell them that you don't want to go". So I went to my recruiter and told him that I did not want to go and his words were "You have to go". Again, being naïve and already dealing with the spirit of rejection and fear, I did not challenge his words. Now for those of you who are reading this book and may have been in the military - know that unless you have been sworn in, you are not obligated and can change your mind. So I went on to boot camp and what happened in boot camp changed my life. God's word is true. He will fulfill His purpose in our lives. Romans 8:28 says, *"And we know that ALL things work together for good to those who love God, to those who are the called according to his purpose"* (NKJ). God used my time in boot camp to show me that I could pray. I would eventually come to embrace the gift that God gave me to pray for others. I want to encourage many of you who are reading this book. You may have made some decisions out of fear that you knew were not right for you, but you went along with it. I am here to remind you that God has a way of taking that very thing and turning it around for your good because you are called according to His purpose. Again, YOU ARE CALLED ACCORDING TO HIS PURPOSE! He has a plan for your life. If you have a sincere heart to serve Him, no amount of mishaps will keep God's divine purpose from manifesting in your life. The things that you have gone through or may be going through right now will work together for your good because you love the Lord. That recruiter was thinking about his purpose for the Army and meeting his quota - but God had already set up a plan that would eventually reveal to me just what it was He called me to do and get me to a place of knowing Him as Lord.

During boot-camp I was miserable. I hated it there and all I wanted to do was go home. Although I had gotten saved at thirteen, I was still lonely and did not truly have a sense of who God was. At that time, He was just God; someone that looked down at me and made sure I did good things and got mad at me when I messed up. I had no clue that He was a caring, loving, righteous creator who wanted the best for my life. He was also the God of peace, restoration, healing and many other wonderful attributes that I have come to know through His word and by the Holy Spirit revealing them to me. I started going to church in basic training and during service, I would feel the pull of His presence upon my heart. I would cry in church and would go back to the barracks, get into my wall locker and pray like I've never prayed before. I wanted so bad to be out of that place. I was praying everywhere I could. I would even go into the bathroom and pray. Every chance I got, I prayed. One night, I remember praying, "God if you get me out of this I will serve you for life". Well, He answered my prayer; I went home in December 1990. He answered my prayers - not because I knew the right words to say, but He answered my prayers because these were prayers that I said from a place of humility and out of desperation from my heart. I was at the end of myself and I turned to Him and He answered my prayers. He will answer your prayers, because He loves you and hears the prayers of your heart. It will not be because you have the right words, but because you are praying from a place of humility. It does not matter what situation you are in. Looking back, being in the military was not that bad but at that time I was already in a vulnerable place. I had a lack of purpose and being there just brought out all the feelings associated with loneliness, sadness and rejection, so I needed to leave. Although I still did not know what was in store for my life when I left the military, God did.

When I returned home I was free but I was still afraid. I know it may sound weird and some may ask, "How can she be free but still afraid"? Well, I was free in a sense that I saw God in a different way. I got the revelation that He does care about me and He does answer prayers, but I was still afraid because I still did not know what I wanted to do in my life. I had no clue of my purpose. As I stated earlier, it would not be until many years later that I would realize that prayer from the marketplace to the church, is the ministry that God called me into. During boot-camp I had witnessed a side of God that I had not seen before. I am taking the time to reveal a part of my life story because I want people to know that your life can be broken and fragmented - leaving you feeling insecure, fearful and with low self-esteem, but your life does not have to remain this way. You don't have to live as a little girl in a woman's body, still dealing with past hurts and disappointments and allow these things to sabotage your purpose and destiny. These are only feelings and these feelings are trying to deceive you into believing that this is who you are and this is who you will always be. I come to tell you that this is not truth, but indeed a lie that needs to be exposed. You are greater than your feelings. You have the power and the authority through Jesus Christ to dictate your feelings and place them under subjection to the word of God. In Psalm 43, King David, spoke to his soul. Verse 5 says; *"Why are you cast down, oh my soul? And why are you disquieted within me? Hope in God; for I shall yet praise Him, the help of my countenance and my God."* The New Living Translation version is really encouraging. *Verse 5 says; "Why am I discouraged? Why is my heart so sad? I will put my hope in God! I will praise him again - my Savior and my God!"* How encouraging is this word! Surely if David can speak to his soul, so can we!

Your past does not have to dictate your future. You belong to

God. Again, you are God's child and you belong to Him. When you trust and believe in His word, you can expect Him to do everything He says He will do. You are not a second-class citizen. You have gifts and talents that God has given you to use as blessings to those around you. Your deliverance is not just for you alone. It is also for other young women and men who need to hear how God built you up in His word and allowed you to stand as you are standing - on the Rock which is Jesus. There is power in His Word and that power will be released through you. Release your life to Him so that He can release His power through you. Don't hold back out of fear. He has called you to be transparent; first with Him so that He can heal you, then with others so that He can use you to bring healing to those who are hurting emotionally. It is through your transparency (if you are willing) that God will use you to build up hurting people and give them a front row seat to the Grace of our Lord Jesus Christ. You may be in the church serving on staff, in the choir, as an usher or even a minister and know in your heart that you have not totally released your life to Him. The secrets you have not told anyone, or even acknowledged to yourself are hindering your ability to be used by God and see all of Him. These secrets need to be exposed. Silence gives the devil power. If there are things in your life that still causes you to feel shame even when you think about them - then this is an indication that healing needs to take place. His desire is to heal you, not hurt or shame you. He wants to make you a strong Woman of God, with the ability to build others up in the things of God and allow them to see that they too have purpose even after experiencing life's hurts and disappointments. You are not alone and God can use you for His Purpose.

STUMBLING ALONG THE WAY

After boot-camp my sister invited me to come and live with her in Colorado Springs, Co. So, I packed up my bags and moved in with her. Although I had an awesome experience with God and saw Him in a new way - I did not pursue a church home to teach me the word of God, so needless to say I began to conform to my environment. I started going to clubs/bars and doing things that even as a teenager I would not engage in. I still knew God, however the life and environment that I came into was one that did not demand the presence of God. I was a babe in Christ and failed to renew my mind with the Word of God. I subjected myself to the plans of the enemy rather than to the plans of our Heavenly Father. But God! He always has a plan even when we think we are so far off. He has a way of calling you in your spirit, even when your natural ears are closed to Him. Although my mind was far from Him, my spirit was yearning for His presence. I remember thinking 'I need to pray', but then I would go about doing what I wanted to do. He was drawing me and calling me but I was not listening. I arrived in Colorado Springs, Co in December 1990 and around August 1991, I was done with the life there. I had met this young man by the name of James Eric Jackson. I remember when I saw him for the first time I said out loud, "That is going to be my husband". I did not know his name, where he came from or anything about him - but something in me just said it so I spoke it. To this day, my sister asks me, "How did you know that he would be your husband"? I told her I did not know anything but just spoke it and what I spoke came to pass. I am so blessed to say that we have been married for twenty-two years this year. Your words are powerful so be careful what you say about others and what you say about yourself. Always make it your priority to speak well of each other. If you feel that you cannot do this, then don't say anything and ask the Lord to help you to be a blessing in word and in your actions.

"*The vision*"

I remember going to bed one night and I had a vision of

angles flying in the clear night sky. It was like they were coming to get me and I woke up and said out loud "I am not ready yet". Even now I can still see the beautiful night sky. It was like God was reminding me that I belonged to Him in this vision. It was so clear that I thought I was actually looking in the sky, only to find out that I was still in my bed. After that vision, I made a decision that I was going to hold tight to the values of God and was not going to be what my environment demanded me to be. From that point on, I had an 'on again off again' relationship with God in my own eyes. At least that is what I thought, but the truth of the matter was that even during those times when I was not pressing into His presence through prayer and reading His word - He was still with me. He never left me but was always living on the inside of me. I now know **Hebrews 13:5** to be so true, *"He Himself said, "I will never leave you nor forsake you".* He stood by my side even when I was not standing with Him. He wanted the best for me and He wants the best for you.

TIME OF RECONNECTION TO THE REDEEMER

Have you ever looked back over your life and asked the question, how did I get here? I often think, 'Where would I be if I had not did this or if I would have done it another way?" I believe we all have these thoughts. These are moments in our life where we are heading in one direction, but because of God's destiny for our life we end up going another way. For myself, I often wonder how could a young lady from Opelousas, Louisiana marry a man from Washington, DC, have 2 wonderful children and end up living in Harrisburg, Pennsylvania. If someone would have told me this when I was 17 years old I would have laughed in their face. Why? Because I could not imagine doing anything successful outside of the environment that I was in at that time. I had no idea that I could ask God questions such as; "What are your plans for my life?" or even "What are my gifts?" Proverbs 29:18 says, "Where there is no vision, the people perish but he that keepeth the law, happy is he". Because I had no vision, my life was filled with no purpose and I was sad - I was sad in my spirit. As I said in the previous chapters, I had no direction in the things of God. The enemy used my sadness to plant a seed of defeat. Some may find it hard to believe - and even I find it hard to believe, that this was my mindset. But in my mid-twenties, I had settled in my mind that serving God was just too hard. The back and forth in serving God was too much and if I ended up in eternal darkness, then so be it. One year I am good and I am saved; the next year I feel like I am so far away from Him, only to start the process all over again. It was a cycle that I was going through and I was frustrated. For a moment, I believed the lie of the enemy that serving God was too much work and I could have more fun in the world. I thought, 'Look at them, they are not serving God and they are happy and not worrying about going to hell, so it must be ok'. WOW! Even now when I think about those thoughts, it makes me mad that I was allowing myself to be deceived by the enemy. I know that there are many out in the world participating in the world's system - not because they don't love the Lord, but because the devil has convinced them to believe the lie that serving our Lord Jesus Christ is too hard. If you are feeling this way, I come to you today to tell you this is a spiritual attack on your life. Ephesians 6:12 says: *"For we are not fighting against flesh-and-blood enemies, but against evil rulers and authorities of the unseen world, against mighty powers in this dark world, and against evil spirits in the heavenly places."* (NLT) If you are not feeling this way but know someone who has believed this lie - stop reading this book and call, text, e-mail or Instagram them and tell them, "God loves you and serving Him is not hard. It is a lie from the enemy'. It is hard when we try and do the Lord's work in our own strength, but with God "All things are Possible". I now know it was hard because I was trying to do it without the leading of the Holy Spirit. I was not living in His Grace. I thought I had to do everything perfect and God would be mad at me if I made a mistake or sinned. Sin does separate us from God. When we truly repent and turn from sin to Him, He embraces us and forgets that we ever sinned. As Believers, we will have trails in this life but we have an advocate who intercedes for us at the right hand of God, which is Jesus Christ. In addition, He sent us the Holy Spirit to give us counsel during these times so that we are able to overcome these trails. During this time in my life, I had no idea of the spiritual attack I was under. Nor did I know that I had the authority to tear down these diabolical thoughts, as well as others through the Word of God. These were thoughts that were coming from the pits of hell; thoughts such as, you are not smart, you cannot change and you will never be anything. These thoughts bombarded my mind and at that time I chose to accept them and they soon became my identity. So accepting the thought that it was too hard to serve God was easy at that time. If I heard a voice say, "You will never be smart enough to get this job", then I accepted that word and did not challenge it with the Word of God. This is why it is so important to read and know the Word of God so that we are able to decree and declare it against the enemy. The word of God is powerful and God wants us to use it in this spiritual war that we are in to destroy generational curses, addictions and all sorts of yokes that have ensnared our lives and are keeping us from fulfilling His purpose.

I felt like I was destined to fail and every time a good thing would happen for me or too me, I would be afraid because I had trained myself to believe that I did not deserve it. Thank you Jesus. He saw my purpose and out of His great love for me, He drew me back into His arms. He knew that the life that I had settled to live out was not the life that He called me to live. Once again, God is so awesome!

One day in 1998, I was going about my day at home and I turned on the television. This lady by the name of Joyce Myers was on. At that time, I had never heard of her but she gave an invitation to rededicate my life to the Lord. I said she gave it to me because this is how I felt. I just knew that she was talking to me. So I got on my knees in my bedroom and repeated the prayer that she prayed. I started going to church again and the Lord Jesus started to show me that I was not destined to perish and go to hell. I was destined to live - not only for me, but for my children (I had just found out I was pregnant with my second child). That was the first word of knowledge that I received from the Lord regarding my life "I was destined to live". I did not know exactly what that meant in its entirety, but I knew that a light was illuminated in my spirit again. My vision was to live for Him and surrender my life totally to Him so that I could fulfill my assignments in His Kingdom.

You may be feeling like you will always be defeated and destined to fail, but I want to decree a word into your spirit, "You are not alone, God is with you and He has a plan for your life". You don't have to accept the thoughts of the enemy. It is not hard to serve God; just believe and He will give you everything you need to contend with the enemy for your purpose. God's word for you is that, **"You are His and**

you have Purpose". God did not just do this for me but He is able and willing to do this for anyone that hears the knock on the doors of your heart and allows Him in. You may feel that your life is worthless because you have made mistakes and people have hurt you, but God can and will redeem you - even from your mistakes and hurts. God is the balm of Gilead (Jeremiah 8:22). Jesus is the great physician and is able to heal you of every emotional pain that keeps you from coming to know Him as your Savior. Your mistakes are not the defining moment of your life. He has a place for you where He will reveal His purpose for your life. He may not reveal it all at once, but as you surrender to Him and remain obedient to His leading, you will get His vision for your life and walk out your purpose to fulfill your destiny in Christ.

If you grew up being a fan of Jesus and not a follower of Jesus, then I encourage you to take a leap of faith and reconnect to your Redeemer. You might be afraid but it is ok, do it anyway. There is a tug on your heart and it is Jesus calling you to Him so that He can give you vision for your life. You are no accident. You are full of purpose. God created you and has given you life so that you can get to know Him as your Redeemer and allow the heart of the Father to flow to you. Do not delay! Today is the day of your Salvation! Even if you have been disconnected from God, please know that He has always been with you. Reconnecting to our Redeemer is possible! The bible says in Romans 8:28, *"That He causes ALL things to work together for the good of those who love Him and are called according to His purpose"*. So even in your mess, He can still use you and the mess for His purpose. He is God and He has the power to change your life in an instant.

Please repeat this Prayer:

Father in the Name of Jesus, I come before you with my heart. I ask that you come into my heart and heal me of past mistakes, hurts and disappointments. I cannot do this on my own and I look to you, my Redeemer, to make a way that I could not and cannot make for myself. Give me a repentant heart so that I can truly turn away from the things that I have allowed to separate me from your love and the revealing of your vision for my life. I love you Lord and I cry out today as a baby cries out to a mother for nourishment and comfort. I know that you are able to do it and I wait with expectation of your presence. In Jesus' Name I pray. Amen

BEING FILLED WITH HIS SPIRIT

On a spring day in 1999, I went to noon-day prayer. We were in a circle praying and one of the Elders looked at me and said, "You are concerned about two things, your husband and being filled with the Holy Spirit." He started to pray and all of a sudden I began to speak in tongues; I will never forget that moment. I don't know what I was praying but I could not stop. I went back to work and was still speaking in the Spirit. I felt like scales had fallen from my eyes and I could see clearer. I cannot even describe to you in detail what that day felt like. It was another level of what I felt at the age of 13. I knew that something had shifted in my life and opened me to another realm of the Lord's power and authority. Being filled with the Holy Spirit exposed the hidden plans of the enemy, but more importantly God showed me the treasures of hidden places. Isaiah 45:3 says, *"And I will give you treasures hidden in the darkness-- secret riches. I will do this so you may know that I am the LORD, the God of Israel, the one who calls you by name."* (NLT) He called me by my name and began to show me the treasures that I had on the inside of me but were hidden by darkness. Although I was saved and accepted Jesus Christ, I still had some dark places in my spirit. When I got filled with the Holy Spirit, it illuminated those dark places and revealed to me my treasures. As Isaiah 45 says, *"He did this so that I may know that it is Him that called me by my name."* What I had just gained access to allowed me to see that the enemy was after my life and my family. It was like the Lord said, "Now I am going to reveal to you just who it is that has been trying to steal your purpose and destiny" and boy did the Holy Spirit reveal!

THE WARFARE; WITH GOD I WIN!

I had just delivered my second son and through a series of events, I thought my husband was having an affair with someone I considered to be my best friend. I was distraught. So distraught, that I could not bond with my newborn baby. All of my attention was on my husband and what he was doing. Through this trial, God showed me that over the years I had given my husband a position in my life that should have been occupied by Him: I had made my husband my God. My entire life at that time, evolved around my husband's needs. I was still dealing with the remnants of insecurity and inferiority. All my attention went to my husband. So when the suspicion of infidelity was revealed to me, I was broken. The thought of my husband seeing someone else - let alone someone I considered a friend, really broke me to pieces. I would cry all the time. Although I knew and loved the Lord, I did not know how to deal with this trial. Boy did I soon learn.

What I learned was how to fight spiritually for my life and my family. I believe God was teaching me two things during this time: (1) How to fight with spiritual weapons and (2) How to love and respect my husband in the proper way - not making him my main focus. God needed me to put my husband in his proper place so that I could put Him (God) where He belonged, which was the Head of my Life. Was this my husband's fault? Of course not. He was unaware of the issues that I had been silently dealing with. He did not know that because of my insecurity and low self-esteem, even thinking that he was cheating on me would cause me to almost lose my mind. He was unaware of the issues that I went through as a young girl, teenager and even as a young adult and how this one incident took me back to a place of brokenness and insecurity. It was like God was saying to me, "I have allowed this to happen to you so that I can show you what I have placed on the inside of you". During this time I prayed, I fasted, I read the Word of God daily and the Lord began to show me things that I had never seen before. Not in my husband's life, but my own life. He was dealing with me on all levels, even leading me to go and apologize to people who I had hurt through gossip and lies. I needed the Lord so much that I did not care what anyone thought about me. The mask came off and I allowed myself to be transparent so that God could heal my inner spirit. So I apologized and asked those people for forgiveness. Day by day, I started to feel better about myself and the situation. I no longer focused on the enemy's thoughts that were coming to me regarding my husband's suspected infidelity, but started to focus on God's word. He began to show me through scripture that I could speak His word and see change and I did see change.

The Lord began to show me in His word that I was worthy of living, that I had a voice and I was not insignificant. I became bold through the word of God and I began to do things that for years I was afraid to do because the devil had convinced me that I was not worthy. I was healed. When I looked in the mirror, I no longer saw insecurity, sadness and fear; I saw a powerful woman of God filled with God's Spirit. I could do anything that God had purposed me to do. During this time I thought I was a mess, but in reality and in truth - I was going through the metamorphic process. God was changing my mindset and giving me stability in Him. Through my brokenness, God brought healing to my soul and I really became a new creature in Christ. I was bold and knew who I was. The old Cynthia was gone. She was no longer a part of my destiny. God not only healed me, but brought me to a new place in my marriage. Was the rumor of his infidelity true? I don't know because I made a decision to shift my focus from what my husband was doing to what God was doing and what God was doing was bigger and better than anything my husband could have done. When God becomes your focus, you just know that He will make all things work together for your good because you made a choice to worship Him and not your situation. I learned during this time that I was called according to His purpose (Romans 8:28) so He would make it work together and He did. My husband and I have been married for twenty-two years this year and we are blessed.

There may be someone reading this book and you might be saying, I am broken in my spirit and I am sad. You are feeling unworthy, lonely and you really don't know who you are. I want to encourage you to press into Jesus. If you don't know Him, ask Him into your life. He will come and abide in you. He will give you everything you need to live the life that He has called you to live. No one can give you what God can give you. How do I know this? Because He created you for His purpose. He has the master plan and the blue prints of your life. Don't give up; don't quit on your life. The enemy wants you to think it is hard but it's not. It is just an illusion that the enemy has placed before you so that you are unable to see the goodness of our Lord Jesus Christ in your life. God loves you with an everlasting love. It does not matter what you have done in the past or what you may go through in the future. He can use that place of pain to give you purpose. Out of your brokenness He can bring healing and a new you will be birthed. I am a living testimony that God can heal your inner turmoil and bring you to a place of power and purpose in His name.

CHOICES ON THE ROAD TO DESTINY

When we were born into this world, we were born into sin. Our very nature automatically becomes a conduit to which every sin imaginable could manifest itself through us. However, it is up to us to ensure that we choose what God has laid out for us through His son Jesus Christ. Life is all about choices and the word of God shows us that God gave us the choice of life when we choose Him. He tells us in His word what will happen when we are obedient and what will happen when we choose to be disobedient. Deuteronomy 30:19 says, *"I call heaven and earth as a witness today against you, that I have set before you life and death, blessing and cursing; therefore choose life, that both you and your descendants may live."* God does not commit strong-armed robbery against us in order for us to be faithful to Him. What He does is reveal everything to us by His Word so that we can see what will be consequences to our choices. There are several scriptures in the bible I could write about that would clearly demonstrate how our choices affect our destiny, but I want to focus on Matthew 15. If you are not familiar with this passage of scripture, please stop reading this book and read it from the Holy Bible. This woman's commitment to her daughter's destiny really ministered to me. The choice she made to stand in the face of insult after insult speaks volumes - not only to her dedication to her daughter, but to her faith in Jesus to fulfill His promise that He is a deliverer. This woman of Canaan made a decision that she was going to intercede for her daughter. She was not going to just let Jesus pass her by without making a healing request for her daughter. Even the disciples were annoyed by her and they even urged Jesus to send her away, but she would not stop. The amazing thing about this scripture is that Jesus was quiet when she first asked Him to heal her daughter. I believe He was quiet because He was making a divine connection with God at that moment to inquire what He was supposed to do in this situation. The bible says in John 5:19, *"Most assuredly, I say to you, the Son cannot do nothing of Himself, but what He sees the Father do; for whatever he does, the Son also does in like manner."*

Although Jesus did not say a word and the disciples tried to write her off, she was persistent in her faith for Jesus to heal her daughter.

"And behold a woman of Canaan came from that region and cried out to Him, saying, 'Have mercy on me, O' Lord, Son of David! My daughter is severely demon-possessed.' But He answered her not a word. And His disciples came and urged Him, saying, 'Send her away, for she cries out after us.' But He answered and said, 'I was not sent except to the lost sheep of the house of Israel.' Then she came and worshiped Him, saying. 'Lord, help me!' But He answered and said, 'It is not good to take the children's bread and throw it to little dogs.' And she said, 'Yes, Lord, yet even the little dogs eat the crumbs which fall from their masters' table.' Then Jesus answered and said to her, 'O woman, great is your faith! Let it be to you as you desire.' And her daughter was healed from that very hour." **Matthew 15:22-28**

She made a choice to not let the spirit of rejection and offenses keep her daughter from receiving her healing and fulfilling her destiny. She could have walked away feeling rejected and put down, but she didn't because her daughter's life was at stake. She could not afford to allow her feelings to get in the way of her daughter's destiny. She made a choice to press on further in spite of their attitudes towards her. This is what contending for your destiny is about. She contended for her daughter's destiny. In faith, she put a demand on the word of God, it was activated and her daughter was healed. Maybe she read the Holy Scripture in Isaiah 11:10; *"And in that day there shall be Root of Jesse, who shall stand as a banner to the people; for the Gentiles shall seek Him and His resting place shall be glorious."* Paul also mentions this scripture again in Romans 15, *"That the Gentiles might glorify God for His mercy."* I believe she had a word from the Lord. The word that she had was truth and truth made her daughter free. The woman just didn't turn around and leave. She had received a word about who Jesus was and she was willing to be insulted and rejected in order to see God's word come to pass. She contended for her daughter with her words to Jesus.

How many times are we to do this very thing? We have the Word of God - so therefore we have life and wherever life is, there is change. It is so important for us to contend for the promises of God for our lives and the lives of others. It does not matter what others say or feel about us; if we believe in Jesus and all the promises He has for us, then it is worth it. Our contending should not depend on if others are for us because in most situations people will be against you. Our contending should come from a place of Faith in Christ and His ability to do what He says He will do. You have the power to alter your destiny through the choices you make daily. Don't allow life to make these choices for you. It is your God-given right - as His child, to accept the choices that He has set before you that will bring you blessings and not curses; that will bring you life and not death. He has already given you the answers to life and they are in His word, which is His Son Jesus Christ.

FOCUS

The definition of focus is to direct toward a particular point or purpose. Our purpose in Christ will require us to stay focused on each assignment that He has called us to fulfill, because each assignment gets us closer to our destiny. It also opens opportunities for those who are connected to us to reach their destiny. There are distractions all around us trying to steal our God opportunities away from us. Our minds are bombarded with the cares of this life and if we are not careful - months, years and even decades could pass by without us even knowing that we have missed pivotal moments that could have advanced the Kingdom of God. It is imperative that we understand the tactics, schemes, plots and plans of Satan. The bible tells us that we ought not to be ignorant of the enemy's devices. His devices have been used for centuries, yet many of us have fallen prey to them. These devices could come in the form of dysfunctional relationships, sickness and idealness. So therefore we have to fight for our God purpose, because this world will not allow you to obtain it without a fight. When I say 'fight' I do not mean in the carnal way, because the bible tells us in Ephesians 6:10-12, *"For we do not wrestle (fight) against flesh and blood, but against principalities, against powers, against rulers of the darkness of this age, against spiritual hosts of wickedness in heavenly places"*.

God - in His love and kindness towards us, not only shows us our enemy but he also tells us how to fight and what weapons we are to use when we engage in contact with the enemy. Ephesians 6:10-18 (NIV) says: *"Finally, be strong in the Lord and in his mighty power. Put on the full armor of God so that you can take your stand against the devil's schemes. For our struggle is not against flesh and blood, but against the rulers, against the authorities, against the powers of this dark world and against the spiritual forces of evil in the heavenly realms. Therefore put on the full armor of God, so that when the day of evil comes, you may be able to stand your ground, and after you have done everything, to stand. Stand firm then, with the belt of truth buckled around your waist, with the breastplate of righteousness in place, and with your feet fitted with the readiness that comes from the gospel of peace. In addition to all this, take up the shield of faith, with which you can extinguish all the flaming arrows of the evil one. Take the helmet of salvation and the sword of the Spirit, which is the word of God. And pray in the Spirit on all occasions with all kinds of prayers and requests. With this in mind, be alert and always keep on praying for all the saints."*

At each level of attack there are methods that God reveals to us to counter-attack and dismantle the enemy's hold. So God - through His word, is showing us how we are to prepare for battle and at each level we are to listen attentively to the direction of the Holy Spirit. The bible says in Romans 8:14, **"For as many are led by the Spirit of God, these are the sons of God."** We have to contend even for our time with the Lord. As soon as you set in your heart to spend time with the Lord, there will be all types of distractions. These distractions are coming strategically to keep you from gaining insight and revelation knowledge of what it is that God has called you to do in each season of your life. He is the one that orders our footsteps. But how can He order our footsteps if we do not have fellowship with Him? It is impossible to get to know someone without communicating with that person. This is the same for Jesus; if we want to know what He has for us then we must focus on Him and spend time in His presence. Even in the natural, a solider does not know where his next assignment is until he receives his orders. He does not just wake up and decide one day that he is going to move to another location. His orders come from a higher-level authority and he moves out at the appointed time they have already predetermined. So therefore, it would be unwise of us to think that we can just live our life without spending time with the Father through His Son Jesus Christ to gain insight to where He is leading us.

Remember our fight is not with our sister, brother, job, wife or husband - but our fight is against one of the entities that Paul mentions in Ephesians 6. In order to contend for our destiny it is going to take us focusing on who God has called us to be and to be led by the Holy Spirit daily. Again, no good solider goes into battle in his own way. A solider that understands warfare knows that there is a level of authority that has access to intelligence that he needs to have in order to destroy the enemy's strongholds. Our higher authority is Jesus Christ: the one who is, who was and is to come. He has given us the Holy Spirit to guide us into all Righteousness and Truth. His Kingdom will never end, so we are to focus on His plan for our life and the lives of those connected to us so that we can win each battle. I cannot give you a formula or '12 steps' on how to keep focus or spend time with Jesus, because this has to come from Him. He has specific times for each of His children, but I will encourage you to be committed to whatever He reveals to you. It is out of commitment that you see the results of His word in your life. Will it be a challenge? Yes it will, but just like every challenge or opposition - we have the power of the most High God to overcome it. The bible tells us this in John16:33 which says, **"In the world you will have tribulation; but be of good cheer, I have overcome the world."** So we are already overcomers of all that would stand in our way. Your willingness to cut everything out and focus on Jesus will bring forth divine revelation and insight to what He is doing in our life and the lives of others.

LIVING FROM THE INSIDE OUT

God has given us the ability to overcome every trial or situation that comes into our lives. He has created within us an internal, spiritual GPS system that will default back to seeking a relationship with Him. Some have chosen to ignore this GPS system and rely on external things to protect them and or help them. The truth is every one of us - as God's children, has been given the desire to seek His face. Living from the inside out means that we don't allow circumstances to dictate our life; we allow the Holy Spirit, which lives on the inside of us to lead and guide us into all righteousness. When trials occur don't allow them to shape us, but take authority over the situation through prayer and allow God to lead us so that we will always have victory over the enemy. Allowing the situation to control us, means that we have made that thing our God and we are living from the 'outside in'. Again I say, if we allow the situation to alter who God has called us to be - we have allowed it to become our God.

God's desire is not for us to turn to others or even ourselves when we are going through trials and tribulations. He may bring great people in your life that will be able to encourage you and assist you, but ultimately He wants us to first turn to Him. He knows everything and everything we need is in His presence. Remember He can see all things from all angles, so when we turn to Him He is able to work His will in our lives; instead of us working our own will or someone else's will in our life. When we allow our problems to become bigger than God in our own eyes, then we give that situation the authority to operate in our life. This is what happened to the children of Israel when they were going over to the promise land (Numbers 14). They believed what they saw in the land of Canaan, rather believing what they heard from God. God told them to go and take possession of the land - but they made a decision to go and spy the land first, which placed fear in some of their hearts. They were living from the outside in, not the inside out. When God gives you a word, do His word. He will not call you to do something that He has not already prepared and equipped you to do. His word does not return to Him void; if He speaks something in your spirit, then move out on it. It is called Faith. You cannot have all the 't's crossed and the 'i's dotted before you do what God has called you to do. You have to move and as you move, God will unfold His plan for your life. Every great inventor moved out on faith. They lived from the inside out, their dreams were bigger than their obstacles and even in the midst of failure - they continued to press on. In spite of others calling them radical, crazy and telling them it will never work, they still pressed on. Because of their pressing we now have airplanes, cars, lights, television, cell phones and so many other things that bring comfort to our lives.

Are you going to continue to press on in spite of your obstacles? Are you going to live from the inside out or the outside in? Your victory over the enemy's plans will require that you don't look at situations and circumstances with your natural eye, but that you look at them from a spiritual perspective. 2 *Corinthians 10:4 says*, *"That our weapons of warfare are not carnal but mighty in God for pulling down strongholds"* Our weapons are mighty in God and we are able to pull down every strong-hold that the enemy sends our way. It is imperative that we receive what God has for us by way of the spirit so that we are able to accomplish His purposes and fulfill His will for this time.

KNOWING GOD LOVES YOU

G od says in His word that He will never leave us or forsake us. This statement is true whether you believe it or not. Jeremiah 31: 3 says, *"Yes, I have loved you with an everlasting love; therefore with love in kindness I have drawn you"*. God created us for a purpose and He has given us every opportunity to find that purpose, in Him. He has already given us the map to access our purpose, which is His word. However it is our responsibility to seek Him so that He is able to reveal it to us. He cannot reveal it if there is no intimacy with Him. James 4:8 says *"Draw near to God and He will draw near to you."* For most of my life I questioned His love towards me and sometimes these thoughts of being unloved by God will rise up again and try to get me to entertain the notion that God does not love me. Fortunately, I have learned through the Word of God that these thoughts are influenced by the God of this world and not from our Father's heart.

God has shown me on many occasions how much He loves me and how much He desires for me to know Him. However, this does not deter the enemy from trying to get me to believe that God does not love me. The enemy is always trying to influence us to believe his word rather than God's word. For this purpose, we are to be steadfast in His presence through the word and prayer so that when these thoughts of uncertainty come our way - we will have the Word of God to us as a weapon against the enemy's lie. God's word is true. We see His word operating in the earth realm every day. When God spoke, *"Let there be light"*; light appeared and no man, devil or principality has ever caused this light to go out. If God says it, it shall surely come to pass. It takes just as much time to believe a lie as it does to believe the truth, so I appeal to you to believe the truth of God's word. He is faithful!

When we make mistakes His mercies are there for us. Nehemiah 9:19 says, *"Yet in your manifold mercies you did not forsake them in the wilderness." We* repent because we have the heart of the Father and it grieves His heart when we walk outside of His will for our life. He has given us a way to come to the throne of Grace to receive forgiveness, when we fall short of His Glory. We can be confident that He is faithful to forgive and to cleanse us of all unrighteousness.

It is our inheritance and we have access to it, but we will not receive it if we don't ask for it. James 4:2 says, *"You do not have because you do not ask."* Ask your father for your inheritance. He loves you and desires that you have access to His peace, joy, prosperity and love. All these belong to those of us who are in Christ Jesus. If you are reading this book and do not know the Lord and Savior Jesus Christ, then you too can have access to this inheritance -all you have to do is receive! Yes, receive Him - Jesus Christ into your life and He will pour out unto you all these things. God is an awesome and loving God. He did not leave us on this earth to fend for ourselves but has given us the Holy Spirit to lead us into all truth. This power has been given to us so that we can walk in victory and defeat the enemy when he comes to tempt, distract and lead us away from the path that God has ordained for us. Jesus Christ died on the Cross, not for us to continue to live a powerless life - but He died so that we can walk in the Power and His Might.

We accept the Lord Jesus Christ as our Savior and give our life to Him so that He is able to lead us and guide us into all righteousness for His name sake. We cannot gain access if there is not representation of the Blood of Jesus Christ. It is the blood of Jesus Christ that was shed for our sins and it is the blood of Jesus that stands against the enemy. When Satan sees the blood of Christ he knows there is no getting around it, so he has to leave. Without this first step we will not be able to walk in total victory.

The relationship between Jesus and mankind has to be intimate and is essential to living a victorious life. God desires for us to walk in complete obedience to Him. It is the prerequisite that we need to do in order for Him to lead us into His purpose. God has a plan for our life and it is to give us hope. Disobedience brings destruction, discouragement and disconnection. God explained it to the children of Israel in Deuteronomy 11:26-27: *"Behold I set before you today a blessing and a curse; the blessing, if you obey the commandments of the Lord your God, which I command you today; and a curse, if you do not obey the commandments of the Lord your God, but turn aside from the way which I command you today, and go after other gods which you have not known"*. This word is still alive and relates to our obedience even today. Our obedience to Him is not something that we adhere to sometimes, but it is a lifestyle. It brings us into a greater fellowship with Him and refreshes our soul.

"Without Faith it is impossible to please Him, for he who comes to God must believe that He is a rewarder of those who diligently seek Him" (Hebrews 11:6). We cannot allow what we see, to doubt what we know. God is faithful and through His word He tells us that when we put our trust in Him, He will never fail us - but we have to believe this. We have to set our face like flint and trust God to do the impossible. Again, James chapter 4 says, **"***We have not because we ask not***"**. Living by faith means that we do not rely on our carnal senses to tell us what is truth; we live by the Word of God and we confess it until it comes to pass. God is awesome and we have to know that nothing is impossible for Him because He holds the position as the only true living God. When we take the limits off of God, we experience new ways to serve Him. We can trust Him for things that seem far off for us to achieve and we build our faith in Him. Isaiah 55:8 says, *"His thoughts are not like your thoughts, Nor your ways my ways, says the Lord"*. So we know from this scripture that we cannot even compare our way of thinking to His; His thoughts are far greater than ours. We cannot even come close in comparison to what He desires to do in our lives. Just knowing that God loves us should be enough, however sometimes it is hard for us to experience

His love because of hurts and disappointments from our past. God is not like man - He truly loves us. His love created us and therefore we have a connection with Him that has the potential to blossom into great things at each stage of our life.

YOUR IDENTITY AND PURPOSE

Purpose is a part of our spiritual DNA and is defined as: "The reason for which something exists". When God created us, He created us with a purpose. He already knew what we would be before we knew our parents. As I stated in the beginning of this book, I was born out of an   adulterous relationship, but God still had purpose for my life. You may be born as a result of an adulterous relationship or even as a result of rape - but God has predestined you for life. Meaning, you are here to live a life of 'Purpose'. Your life matters; you are not a tragedy, accident or a burden. It does not matter what others have said about your life. This is only their narrow view and their knowledge is limited. God knows all things. He knows the beginning and the end. He knows how to get us from where we are to where we need to be.

Knowing who you are in Christ is so important because there are constant images from the media and the world that are trying to deceive us and make us believe that who God has called us to be, is second to what the world has portrayed. Their version of us is counterfeit and is way below God's standards. We were destined to reign with Him. Being who God called you and me to be without conforming to this world, can be a challenge. However through Christ we can do all things and that includes - but not limited to, accessing our identity and living it out for the Glory of God. As women we are especially prone to accepting false images from the media around us. However, we don't have to conform to these images in order for us to be accepted or to find out who we are. All we have to do is turn to God and allow His purpose to unfold in our life. The unfolding happens simultaneously when we go after God with all of our heart. He begins to show us what He has placed on the inside and how these things can be used to not only edify the Kingdom of God - but how they can also be used in the market place. Knowing who you are in Christ allows us to be free to give our gifts and talents without any concerns of being rejected. Even if we are rejected, it will not stop us from believing in what God has called us to do and believing in whom God has created us to be. We will just look for the next opportunity or door to open from God that will allow us to express His purpose for our lives and love others in the process.

As women we have to know and learn from an early age that we have purpose. From a very young age, I always compared myself to others that were around me. I noticed that when I met someone I would start to like the same things they liked or I would start to speak like them. I never really knew who I was, so I conformed to those around me. I thought it was normal to be like everyone else, but what I did not realize was that I had an identity crisis. I did not know Cynthia or why I was even placed on this earth. I was never taught nor was it ever explained to me that I had purpose and I was unique in God's sight. It was not until I had that encounter with my loving God in 1999, that I realized God created me to be unique and that I had a purpose for being here on this earth. Before then, I was a lonely young lady looking for acceptance in all the wrong places. Trying to fit in with people that were not called to be in my life and allowing these relationships to remain for fear of rejection. If you have ever felt like this or you may be feeling like this right now, know that God has a purpose for you and you were not created just to exist. You are not lonely nor are you barren in the things of God. You were created to be great and do great things for God! It is your inheritance to find out who you are in Christ and what it is that He has called you to be. Long gone are your times for accepting everyone else's view of yourself. Through Christ He is able to reveal who you are and what He has created you to be. You are not the last; you are the first. You are not the tail; you are the head. Your identity is in Christ and He is eager to show himself strong to you. 2 Chronicles 16:9 says, **"For the eyes of the Lord run to and fro throughout the whole earth, to show himself strong on behalf of those whose heart is loyal to Him."** He is looking for you so that He can show you who you are in Him. Let Him look no longer and allow Him to reveal to you who you really are; **"Who He created you to be, which is fearfully and wonderfully made in His image."** Psalm 139:14

STANDING THE TEST OF TIME

What do we do when our lives are comprised of failure after failure? A lot of times we see situations and circumstances from our own perspective. We allow our own interpretation of time to discourage us and lead us to believe that God has forgotten about us. I am here to inform you that God is greater than time and as a matter of fact, He created time. He has not forgotten about us and His purpose for His life. God created time so therefore He has the ability to suspend it. Joshua 10:12 says, *"Then Joshua spoke to the LORD in the day when the LORD delivered up the Amorites before the sons of Israel, and he said in the sight of Israel, "O sun, stand still at Gibeon, And O moon in the valley of Aijalon." So the sun stood still, and*

the moon stopped, until the nation avenged themselves of their enemies. "Verse 14; "And there was no day like that before it or after it that the LORD hearkened unto the voice of a man: for the LORD fought for Israel."

God answered Joshua's prayer; the sun and the moon stood still. It was a request that God granted because He had the ability to do so. This is why He is God. There is no battle in our life that God has not already given us victory over. Just like Joshua, all we have to do is ask Him to do what He has already willed for our life. He has ordained salvation, healing, breakthrough, destruction of yokes and kingdom assignments. All of these things can be accomplished in our life at the appointed time that Jesus has ordained before the foundations of this earth. Our age does not cancel out our purpose, neither does our struggles. God used Sarah and Abraham well into their senior years to birth a nation (Genesis 15). In God's perfect timing He revealed His plans to Abram and He will reveal His plan for your life also. You have made it this far with the Lord and there is no need for you to use your age as a reason to not believe that God will fulfill His purpose in your life. I would like to prophesy to the person reading this book; your life is not over. You still have gifts and talents that God has placed on the inside of you that will benefit His Kingdom. You have stood the test of time and you are still here. Keep trusting in His word; it is true and He is faithful. Your life is not over. Position yourself through prayer and ask the Lord to reveal His assignments for you in this season that will facilitate your purpose and bring it into manifestation. Ask and it shall be given to you (Matthew 7:7). Yes, to you! Why you? Because He loves you and does not look at what you cannot do, but what you can do in His strength. You can stand the test of time because He has time and you in His hands. Go forth in spite of the failures; go forth in spite of the disappointments and rejection. You are not alone in this life. He is with you. God is a God of second chances. You may have made mistakes in your life, but we all have. We were created with fortitude and determination. It is already in us, ready to be released and all we have to do is access it and release it. Matthew 16:19 say, *"And I will give you the keys of the Kingdom of Heaven and whatsoever you bind on earth will be bound in Heaven, and whatever you loose on earth will be loosed in Heaven"*. Jesus was telling this to Peter and He is also telling us that because we have chosen to accept who He is - which the Son of God is, He will give us the "Keys of the Kingdom of Heaven". This means that He has given us the authority to move things in heaven and in the earth realm. We have this access when we accept Jesus Christ as our Savior. We are able to stand the test of time because we have the keys of the kingdom of heaven. Tell the enemy that you have the authority to push back his works and bind up his plans and tactics against your life and the lives of your loved ones and lose God's divine plan so that He can receive the glory and the honor in our lives.

I ask that you pray this prayer:

Father in the Name of Jesus Christ, I thank you for giving me everything I need to live a life that is pleasing in your sight. I understand that you have given me great authority and power to unlock things that will allow me to stand the test of time and fulfill the assignments that you have ordained for me to fulfill before the foundation of this world. I decree and declare that I will not succumb to weariness and even when I am tired, I will always turn to you so that you can refresh me and remind me of who you are and what you are able to do in my life.

In Jesus' Name I pray! Amen

YOU CAN CONTEND AND WIN!

Finding your Purpose through Life's Trials is the subtitle of this book. I truly believe that we find out who we really are and what we are called to do when we go through the trials of this life. It is through these trials that we are drawn to trust in our creator, the only true living God Jehovah through his son Jesus Christ. We reach outside of ourselves to find ourselves in Christ. It is uncomfortable and does not feel good when we are going through the trial, but God will allow us to see that the process was necessary for the purpose. Again, I say the 'Process was necessary for your purpose to be revealed'. I found my purpose through tears, heartache and pain. But I tell you, I would not change one thing that I had to go through to be in the place where I am today. I love the Lord, I trust the Lord and I am totally committed to His will for my life. Even when I make a mistake and fall short of what He has called me to do; I know that He loves me and gives me strength to repent and turn away from that which I have fallen short in and run to Him.

I shared some of my life struggles in this book because I want every person who is called to read this book to know that life can try and dictate who you are and what you have been called do, but only the Lord has your Purpose and Destiny secured. He knows the richness of who you are and all that He has created you to be and do. Psalm 16:5 says, *"O' Lord You are the portion of my inheritance and my cup. You maintain my Lot."* Another word for 'lot' is 'Destiny'. So this is how I say this scripture, "Lord, you maintain my Destiny". It is God who maintains our destiny; it is not our supervisor, our friends, our spouses or even us - but it is God. Romans 8:30 says, **"Whom he predestined, these He also called; whom He called, these He also justified; and whom He justified, these He also glorified."** (NKV) So God has predestined you, called you, justified you and your life will glorify Him.

I pray that this book revealed to you that God loves you very much and He has not forgotten about your purpose and destiny. God has equipped you with gifts, talents and every spiritual weapon to overcome the plans of the enemy. He had Victory in mind when He created you, not defeat. May God bless you and keep you in His Presence. May you allow the Lord to speak to your spirit and that you embrace what He reveals so that you may become strong in the Lord and in the power of His Might. In His Strength you can do all things! In Christ, you are contending and winning!

To correspond with

Cynthia B. Jackson or for speaking

engagements please send all inquiries

to

cynthia@prayingforchange.org

23901098R00049

Made in the USA
Middletown, DE
07 September 2015